The Little Leonardo da Vinci

Catherine de Duve

Find out about the life of the Renaissance genius

At the time of Leonardo da Vinci

The Renaissance

While Europe is still deep in the Middle Ages, Italy enters a new era, with the flourishing of science and the arts. People rediscover the art of Ancient Greece and Rome. This is the Renaissance. It starts in Italy in the 'Trecento' (1300), carries on in the 'Quattrocento' (1400) and then spreads to the rest of Europe.

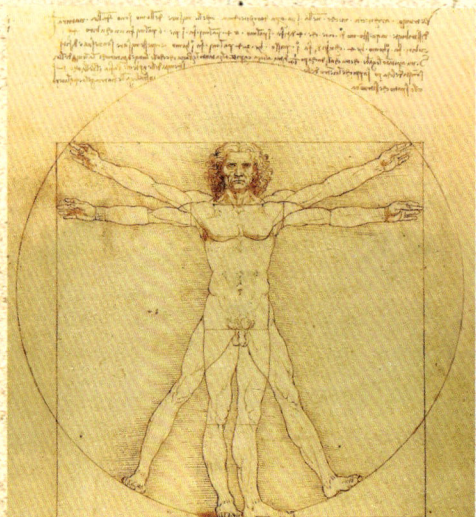

Man is at the centre of the world.

Humanism

Renaissance man has a thirst for knowledge about the world. Scholars study astronomy (the planets and stars) and anatomy (dissection and research to study and understand the human body).

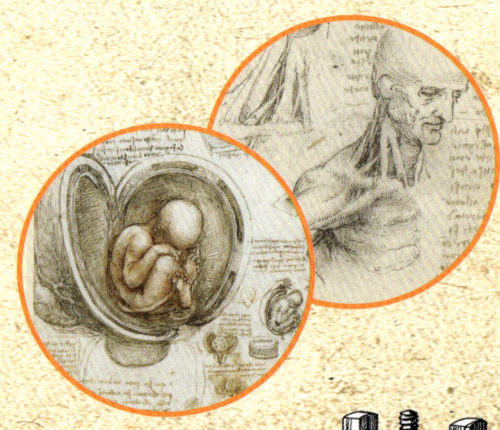

Printing

Thanks to Gutenberg, who, in 1440, invented the printing press, printing becomes more widespread. Books are printed and acquired by wealthy individuals and universities. Leonardo learns and studies from the first printed books.

The Medici Family

In Italy, the city of Florence in Tuscany is prosperous; this is where the Renaissance begins.

Florence, on the River Arno, has more than 100,000 inhabitants. The city has its own currency, called the florin. **Prince Lorenzo de' Medici**, 'the Magnificent', rules there. He's a patron of the arts. He commissions sculptures and decors from Leonardo.

At that time, Italy is made up of various principalities and states. The main cities are Venice, Milan, Florence, Naples and the church-ruled states. These cities war with each other, and other countries become involved in these conflicts.

Who are the great artists of the Italian Renaissance?

Da Vinci   Botticelli   Michelangelo   Raphael

Leonardo da Vinci

How can man fly?

Leonardo da Vinci is born on April 15th, 1452 in Vinci, in the Tuscan countryside, a few kilometres from Florence in Italy. He's the illegitimate son of Ser Piero da Vinci, a lawyer in Pisa and Florence. His father does not marry Caterina, his mother, but, instead, another girl from a rich family.

The little boy lives with his mother, who marries a man of humble origins. In school, Leonardo doesn't learn Greek or Latin. He's fascinated by nature and animals, and plays the lyre. He observes nature, which becomes an endless source of inspiration for him. He watches the birds, their wings and how they move.

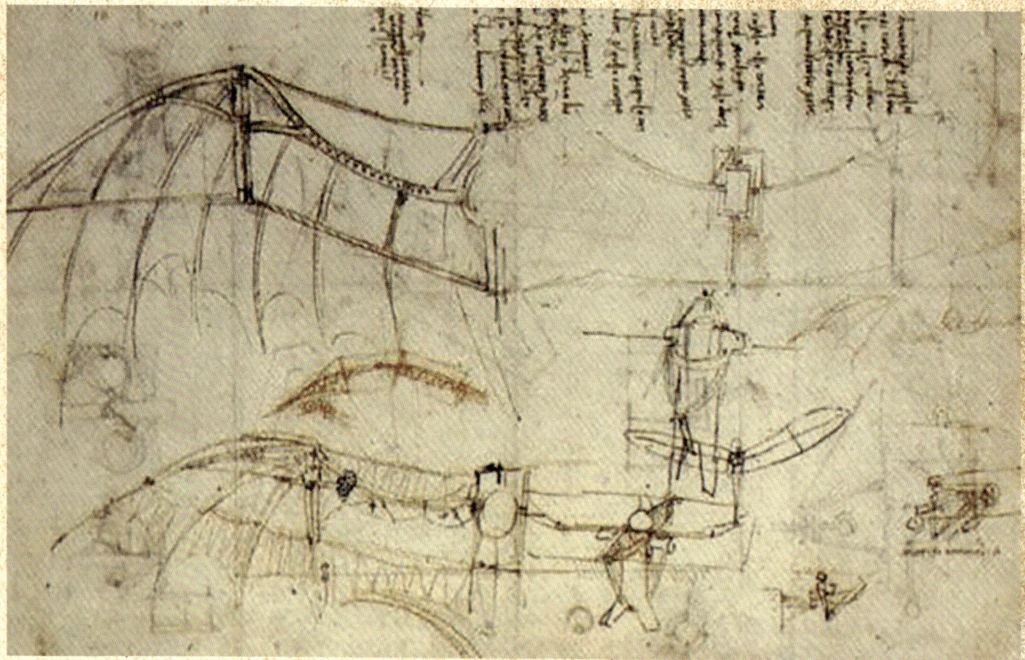

Bottega

Thanks to his father's contacts, the young Leonardo moves to Florence and, in 1469, becomes an apprentice in the studio of the famous painter, sculptor and goldsmith **Verrocchio** (1435-1488). Leonardo draws from nature or copies models by old masters. He also learns sculpture, engraving and jewellery-making, as well as performing many other tasks.

What does an apprentice do in a master's studio?

The 'bottega' (studio in Italian) is buzzing with life. There's lots to do! The apprentices prepare the colours: they crush the pigments. They also prepare the glues and coatings for the wooden supports – willow or linden panels.
They clean the brushes and tools, run errands, light and tend the fire in the kiln.

Budding engineer

The apprentices also make everything needed, such as all sorts of machines (engineering) - especially those used to hoist up the sculptures in the churches.

Verrocchio's studio is commissioned to work on the dome of Florence cathedral, designed by the architect **Brunelleschi** (1377-1446). They must decorate the top of the lantern with copper and gold. How will they lift it back up, afterwards? They have to design machines... Leonardo turns out to be a good inventor and engineer: he designs complex machinery.

Verrocchio

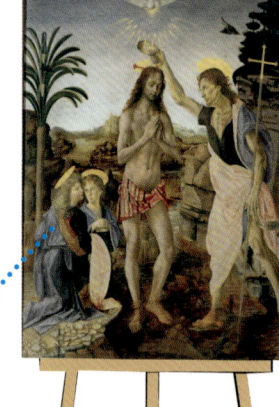

In the studio, apprentices work on the master's commissions, such as this picture, the *Baptism of Christ*.

An angel passing...

According to **Vasari**, the first art historian (1511-1574), Leonardo is 20 when he helps with some of his master's commissions. In this picture, the apprentice paints one of the angels so beautifully that Verrocchio 'despaired since the young man painted better than he did, and gave up painting for ever'.

In 1472, Leonardo joins the association of Florentine painters, the *Compagnia di San Luca*. He paints his first pictures and opens a studio in 1473.

Verrocchio's *David*, in bronze

A handsome model!

In around 1473, Verrocchio creates this sculpture, showing David who has just cut off the head of his enemy, the giant Goliath. It is thought that his model was his blond, curly-haired apprentice: the young, good-looking Leonardo.

Botticelli

In 1478, Leonardo and his friend **Sandro Botticelli** open a tavern: *'Sandro and Leonardo's Three Frogs'*. It's said that the two friends, who met at Verrocchio's studio, decide to open their own restaurant, which closes a few months later. This brief experience, however, inspires Leonardo to invent machines and utensils to save cooking-time.

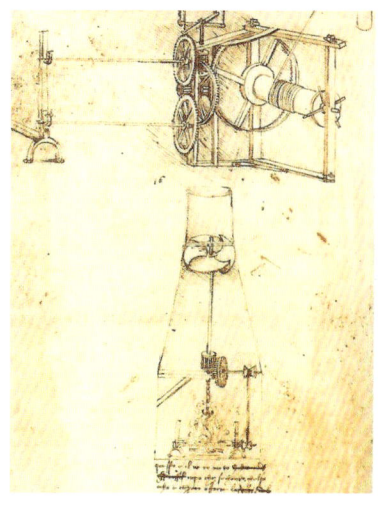

This is the roasting-spit invented by Leonardo.

Sandro Botticelli
1445-1510

Botticelli, the son of a tanner from Florence, is apprenticed to the monk Lippi. He receives his first public commission in 1470 and opens his own studio. In 1481, he paints frescoes for the Sistine Chapel in Rome. His most famous picture is the *Birth of Venus*, painted in around 1485.

The painter dies poor. He has become a follower of the monk **Savonarola**, who burned artworks and objects linked to spiritual corruption, including Botticelli's paintings.

Leonardo the painter

Leonardo paints this picture when he's around 20 and still working in Verrocchio's studio. It's an early, large-scale work (98 x 217 cm). The painter changes some details several times (second thoughts). Some colours have been rubbed by hand, a technique used by the young Leonardo.

- Cypresses and pines
- Meadow in flower: symbol of the town of Nazareth
- White lily: symbol of purity
- Garden enclosed by a low wall (*Hortus conclusus*): symbol of the Virgin's virginity
- Way into the garden
- River landscape

The Annunciation

The Angel Gabriel announces to Mary that she will be the mother of the son of God. Mary, who was reading the Bible, keeps her hand on the page.

Atmospheric view: the blue mountains fade into the horizon

The port: symbol of Mary leading the lost to the safe harbour of eternal salvation

Bible

Halo

Lectern: inspired by a sarcophagus

Duke of Milan

Military engineer

sketch for a cannon

Milan

Leonardo needs a patron (a protector) who will give him the means to paint his pictures and continue his research. He lives from his work and takes on commissions. He moves to another city, Milan. There, the duke of Milan, **Ludovico Sforza**, 'the Moor', aims to supplant the city of Florence and the Medicis.

Leonardo is 30 when he sends a letter to the duke of Milan, offering him his services as a military engineer. He has many ideas, he says, for war machines. He can also build strong, lightweight bridges, drain water from ditches to besiege a stronghold, construct easy-to-transport cannons, dig underground tunnels and secret passages, build unassailable tanks, catapults and vessels, and, in peacetime, he can build public and private buildings, as well as painting and sculpting.

Leonardo devises many attack and defence systems.

First tank

Leonardo sketches one of his inventions, an assault tank with cannons all the way round, so it can shoot in all directions.
Here it is in action.

Here you can see how the wheels work.

Inventions

Daring

Leonardo does his own experiments. He has loads of ideas! He designs various projects, hydraulic systems and all sorts of machines. He's also interested in anatomy, clockwork and architecture.

Party planner

Leonardo loves the good life! He organises sumptuous parties for the Court. He designs decors and costumes for the wedding procession of **Ludovico Sforza** and **Beatrice d'Este**. He also organises games to entertain the Court. He becomes indispensable!

Throughout his life, Leonardo likes to observe nature. Could this be the forerunner of the helicopter?

Portraits, in more detail

At the time, portraits are painted in profile. Leonardo thinks up a new way to paint portraits, with the model at a three-quarter angle. He thus renews the genre.
He receives a commission to paint the duke's mistress.
This elegant portrait is the first not to show the sitter in profile.

The beautiful **Cecilia Gallerani** turns her head to the left and is bathed in light, as is the white stoat in her arms. Her hand is gracefully stroking the animal. Their heads are turned towards the viewer, but they are looking elsewhere. This creates an air of mystery.

Stoat

The stoat, with its white summer coat, can symbolise purity, and is also the duke's emblem.
In Greek, 'gala', as in 'Gallerani', means stoat.

The picture is 54 cm x 39 cm. It's painted on walnut wood, from the same trunk as another picture Leonardo painted in the same year.

Portrait in profile

Three-quarter portrait

In this portrait, the head is looking almost straight at us, while the body is practically in profile. This makes for a very lively picture.

Humanism

The human body

Leonardo makes many studies of the proportions of the human body.
The Vitruvian Man (named after the Roman architect) shows a naked man drawn in two different positions. Leonardo studies the ideal proportions of the human body. The man is set in two perfect shapes, a square and a circle, representing the ideals of symmetry and harmony. Sixteen possible combinations are shown.

Vitruvius

Before Leonardo, the Roman (first-century) architect **Vitruvius** wrote a treatise on architecture, 'De Architectura', which is republished with the development of printing. In it, the architect explains the standard proportions and symmetries of buildings and of the human body. For example, the ratio of face to body is 1:10, although for Leonardo, who studies the human body in detail, the proportion is actually 1:8.

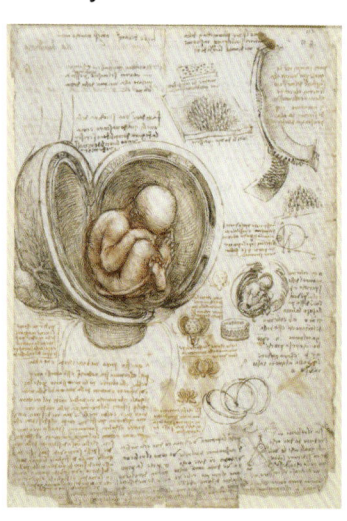

Anatomy

Leonardo is interested in anatomy, and in how the muscles and organs work. He dissects corpses to understand the workings of the human body. He also studies embryology, particularly the development of the human fœtus.

Is the man moving?
How many geometrical shapes can we see?
Leonardo pays attention to the layout
of his drawings and notes.

Heresy

Leonardo is accused of heresy, as Pope Leo X condemns 'natural philosophers' who do not believe in the immortality of the soul.

Mirror writing

What a mysterious writing! Leonardo writes back-to-front and from right to left.

The Last Supper

In 1495, Leonardo begins this fresco to decorate the refectory of the Convent of Santa Maria delle Grazie in Milan.

Supper: evening meal (in Latin, 'cena').

This is the *Last Supper*, Jesus's last meal before his death. His disciples are gathered around him: the twelve apostles.

One of you will betray me.

Composition

Christ is at the vanishing point. At each side are two groups of apostles (four sub-groups, each of three people) with particular feelings, echoing each other. The overall effect is one of perfect unity. The coffered ceiling and tapestries frame the scene. But behind Christ, three windows reveal a mountain landscape and blue sky.

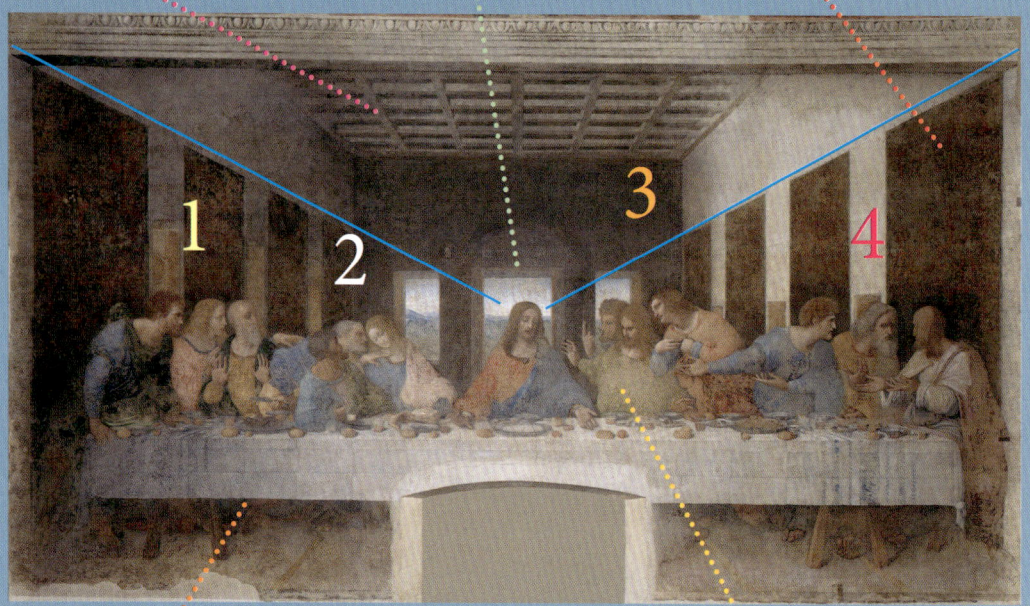

The table

The table, a plank on trestles covered with a white tablecloth, slopes towards us to show what's on it.
What are they eating?
It's a frugal meal.

Monumental

The fresco measures 4.6 x 8.8m. The figures are larger, proportionately, than the other objects in the room, which highlights their importance.

Technique

The painting looks faded - it has been exposed to damp.
Many details and colours have disappeared.

Tempera sur gesso

The technique used is 'tempera', a mix of oil and pigments, on dry plaster. The colours faded quickly. This painting has been restored several times.

What is happening around the table?

Leonardo has chosen to show a tragic moment. Jesus, looking down and open-handed, tells his disciples that one of them will betray him. They are all aghast and react spontaneously to his declaration. We can sense strong emotions and agitation. Who is the traitor at the table? Each disciple reacts in his own way.

Who are these people?

Bartholomew, James, son of Alphaeus, and Andrew.

Judas, who was paid 30 pieces of silver to hand Christ over to the Roman authorities, is talking with Peter and John.

Thomas, James the Greater and Philip.

Matthew gestures towards Christ, while speaking to Thaddeus (or Jude) and Simon.

Body language: hands, feet and eyes

The hands are very expressive. The gestures give drama and movement to the scene. The figures communicate without words. The faces also express emotions.

Equestrian statue

Leonardo plans a monumental statue in commemoration of **Ludovico Sforza**'s father. But in 1494 Italy is invaded by the King of France, **Charles VIII**, and the idea is abandoned. The bronze intended for the statue is used for cannons.

Study of a horse by Leonardo, ca. 1490

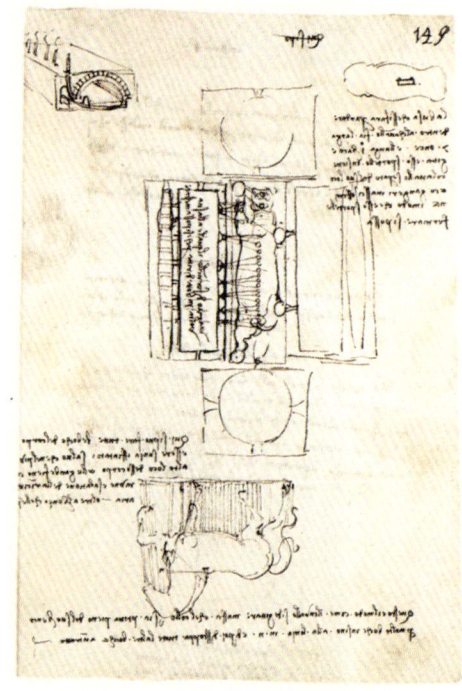

Sketches of the monument for Ludovico Sforza

In 1499, the Duchy of Milan is invaded by the troops of Louis XII, successor to Charles VIII.

Leonardo has to return to Florence. In the meantime, he stops in Mantua, where he paints the portrait of **Isabella d'Este** and her sister, the Duchess of Milan. He then stops in Venice in March 1500, where he works on hydraulic projects.

On his return, Florence has changed. The Medicis have been deposed and the city is now a Republic.

..... *Atmospheric view*

..... **Saint Anne:** Mary's mother. She is a monumental figure, taking up three quarters of the picture. Her daughter sits on her knee.

..... **Mary:** she leans lovingly towards her son Jesus, taking him in her arms. The gestures and gazes of the two mothers echo each other.

..... **Jesus:** the child looks at Mary while playing with a lamb.

..... **Composition:** a complex, dynamic pyramid.

..... **Lamb:** symbol of sacrifice, foretelling the sacrifice of Jesus.

Preparatory drawings

At the same time, Leonardo works on preparatory studies for the *Virgin and Child with Saint Anne*. He gathers together his drawings (feet, drapery, etc.) to compose his ambitious picture.

Cesare Borgia

In 1502, Leonardo begins working for the powerful, feared **Cesare Borgia**, duke of Valentinois, as an architect and engineer.

His job is to inspect cities and fortifications. He draws up records and topographical maps.
He devises new defence systems, such as covered roads, towers and ditches. In particular, he develops plans to divert the River Arno.

Hydraulic machine thought up by Leonardo.

Close-up on the Mona Lisa, 1503

Who is Mona Lisa?

Mona Lisa (1479-1542) is short for Madonna Lisa (Madame Lisa). Her other name, 'La Gioconda', means la *donna* de Giocondo, Giocondo's wife.

Secret masterpiece

Donna Gioconda is married to **Francesco del Giocondo**, a cloth and silk merchant based in Florence. In 1503, the couple move to a new house. Leonardo never actually delivered the finished portrait. He kept it until he died. Mona Lisa herself probably never saw it.

The most famous picture in the world!

Vinci never actually delivered the picture. He kept it with him for the rest of his life. He even crossed the Alps on a mule with the portrait in his bag : he must love it very much! This portrait is so delicately-painted, so mysterious: a masterpiece.

In 1911, the Mona Lisa is stolen!

In August 1911, the picture is stolen. In December 1956, a visitor throws a stone at the glass covering the picture. Since 1974, the *Mona Lisa* is displayed in a bulletproof glass case, in a controlled climate.

Technique

Sfumato
From the Italian 'sfumare': to fill with smoke. Some of the outlines are blurred like smoke. The features of the face, such as the lips and eyelids, are not in clear focus. This creates a mysterious and melancholic effect.

Gaze
Her eyes gaze at us and seem to follow us around.

Support
The picture is painted on a poplar wood panel (77 x 53 cm), often used in Italy.

Oil painting
A mix of pigments (colours) and drying oil.

Smile
Mona Lisa is sitting in front of an imaginary landscape. A faint enigmatic smile plays on her lips.

Landscape
The landscape in the background provides movement. We see imaginary mountains and a winding, shimmering path.

Glazes
Thin layers of transparent oil paint, superimposed. They are slightly tinted with pigments and give the picture depth.

Patterns
Her clothes are austere and dark, and she wears no jewels. Her bodice, embroidered with silk thread, is patterned with diamond-shapes and crosses.

Chiaroscuro
An area where the contrast between light and dark makes shapes stand out. Leonardo is one of the first to use this technique.

Drapery
The folds in the clothing are drawn in sharp focus and contrast with the more blurred parts of the picture.

Fresco

Palazzo Vecchio

Leonardo returns from Milan to Florence. In October 1503, the year the Mona Lisa is painted, the city of Florence commissions Leonardo to produce a huge fresco to decorate the Council room in the Palazzo della Signoria, now the Palazzo Vecchio, an imposing fortress and the seat of the government.

Battle of Anghiari

Leonardo begins the fresco of 'The Battle of Anghiari', commemorating the victory of the Florentines over the people of Milan (1440). He moves to the Monastery of Santa Maria Novella, where he sets up a studio and living quarters.

Leonardo works intermittently on his fresco. Another artist joins him to paint the opposite wall: the young **Michelangelo**. Neither of them finish their frescoes.

Wet paint!

Leonardo paints his fresco with oil paints, but it doesn't dry.
He lights fires to dry the paint, but the upper colours run in the heat.
What a disaster!

 Leonardo's version (1503) and Rubens' version* (1603) of the Battle.

Da Vinci

Rubens

* To find out more, take a look at 'The Little Rubens' in the same collection.

Raphael

Rome

In 1513, the French, defeated, withdraw from Milan, and **Maximilian Sforza**, son of Ludovico, returns to power. Compromised by his links with Louis XII, Leonardo leaves Milan and begins to work for **Giuliano de' Medici** in Rome.

In September 1513, Leonardo leaves for Rome. He settles in the Vatican where **Giovanni de' Medici**, his patron's brother, has become **Pope Leo X**. There, Raphael and Michelangelo are working hard. Leonardo is disappointed, as he is not given work suited to his genius. He is discouraged, and finds it hard to finish what he's started, as is often the case…

Portrait of Pope Leo X, painted by Raphael between 1518 and 1520.

Raphael 1483-1520

Raphael is the son of the official painter of the duke of Urbino. At 17, he becomes apprenticed to Perugino. He takes over his father's workshop. At 21 he arrives in Florence and discovers Michelangelo and Leonardo, whose studio he visits. He then works in Rome for Pope Julius II, then for his successor Leo X. He works with many assistants, sometimes up to 50! He has a graceful, colourful style. He dies from malaria at the age of 37.

Michelangelo

Michelangelo 1475-1564

David, between 1501-1504

Born in Caprese in Tuscany (Republic of Florence), Michelangelo is the son of an important magistrate. He is sent to be looked after by a stonecutter, where he learns to dress blocks of stone. He is apprenticed to **Ghirlandaio**. He copies **Masaccio**'s frescoes. Others envy his talent. He becomes a protégé of Lorenzo de' Medici. He admires Ancient Greek sculptures. He goes to Bologna, then in 1496 to Rome, where he sculpts the *Pietà*. He then returns to Florence and creates the statue of David before going back to Rome in 1505. He has been asked to make Pope Julius II's tomb. Later, he paints frescoes in the Sistine Chapel (1508-1512). He dies in Rome at the age of 88.

Michelangelo paints and sculpts magnificent monumental nudes. He stands out from other artists of the time because of his style, as the power of the bodies shows the heroism of man in action. Here is the *Creation of Adam*, circa 1511.

Clos Lucé Manor

Leonardo's final home

On January 25th, 1515, Francis I is consecrated King of France.
In 1516, after the death of Giuliano de' Medici, Leonardo leaves Italy for France, at the invitation of the King.

Leonardo, now 64, crosses the Alps on a mule with his assistant-painter Francesco Melzi. He sets up home in Cloux Manor, known from then on as Clos Lucé, not far from the Royal Chateau of Amboise, where the King spent his childhood. It's said that the two houses were linked by an underground passage. Leonardo is appointed 'First Painter and Engineer and Architect to the King'. He receives an allowance of 1,000 ecus per year. At last, Leonardo is recognised as an artist, not just as an engineer. As he did in Italy, Leonardo organises sumptuous parties for the Court.

Marignan 1515

In September 1515, the new King of France reconquers Milan. During the peace talks between Leo X and Francis I, the King commissions Leonardo to create a mechanical lion which opens up to reveal lilies, the symbols of his new power. What an effect!

Leonardo's bedroom in Clos Lucé

Leonardo brings three canvasses with him to France.

Saint John the Baptist

The Virgin and Child with Saint Anne

The Mona Lisa

Francis I

You will be free, here, to dream, think and work.

In 1517, Leonardo imagines building a palace at Romorantin, where he plans to divert the course of a river. He designs a canal between the rivers Loire and Saune. Francis I sees Leonardo as a father-figure, but the artist's health is failing and he draws up a will.

Leonardo da Vinci dies on May 2nd, 1519 in Clos Lucé at the age of 67 He is buried in the Chateau of Amboise.

A painter, anatomist, engineer, inventor and architect. Today, Leonardo da Vinci is considered a genius.

Legend has it that Leonardo died in the arms of Francis I. The painter Ingres (1780-1867) imagined the scene.

Text: Catherine de Duve
Concept and editorial coordination: Kate'Art Editions
Layout: Julie Brousmiche
Translation: Rachel Cowler

PHOTOGRAPHIC CREDITS:

Da Vinci: Krakow: Czartoryskis Museum: *Lady with an Ermine or Portrait of Cecilia Gallerani*, ca. 1483-1490: p.13 | **Florence: Uffizi Gallery:** *Annunciation*, 1473-1475: p.8-9; *The Battle of Anghiari*, 1503-1505: p.27 | **London: Royal Collection:** *Study of the foetus in the womb*, ca. 1510: p.2, p.15; *Study of the monument for Sforza*, ca. 1485-1490: p.20 | **London: British Museum:** *Drawing of an armoured tank*, ca. 1485: p.10; *Design for a siege tower with a covered bridge*, ca. 1480: p.10 | **Madrid: National Library:** *Manuscript page on the Sforza monument*, ca. 1493: p.20 | **Milan: Biblioteca Ambrosiana:** *Roasting-spit using weights and air*, s.d.: p.7; *Sketch of a hydraulic system*, ca. 1480-1482: p.23 | **Milan: Convent of Santa Maria delle Grazie:** *The Last Supper*, 1495-1498: p.16-17 (whole), p.18 (whole), p.19 (details) | **Paris: Musée du Louvre:** *Mona Lisa*, ca. 1503-1506: cover, p.3, p.25, p.26, p.30; *La Belle Ferronniere or Portrait of an Unknown Woman*, ca. 1495-1499 - p.12; *Portrait of Isabella d'Este*, ca. 1499-1500 p.21; *The Virgin and Child with Saint Anne*, ca. 1500-1513: p.22, p.30; *Saint John the Baptist*, ca. 1513-1516: p.30 | **Paris: Institut de France:** *Design for a flying machine*, ca. 1488: p.4; *The Architronito*, ca. 1488-1497: p.10; *Studies of central plan buildings*, ca. 1480: p.11; *The Aerial screw*, ca. 1487-1490: p.11 | **Turin: Royal Library:** *Portrait of a man in red chalk*, ca. 1510-1515: p.1, p.3 | **Venice: Gallerie dell'Accademia:** *Vitruvian Man*, ca. 1492: p.2, p.15 | **Windsor Castle: Royal Library:** *Superficial anatomy of the shoulder and neck*, ca. 1510-1511: p.2; *Study of horses*, ca. 1490: p.20 | **Private collection:** *The Beautiful Princess*, 1495: p.12.

Michelangelo: Florence: Galleria dell'Accademia: *David*, 1501-1504 - p.29 | **Rome: Sistine Chapel:** *The Creation of Adam*, 1508-1512: p.3, p.29.

Botticelli: Florence: Uffizi Gallery: *Adoration of the Magi*, ca. 1475: p.3, p.7; *The Birth of Venus*, 1483-1485: p.3, p.7.

Raphael: Florence: Uffizi Gallery: *Self-portrait*, 1506: p.3, p.28; *Portrait of Pope Leo X with Cardinals Giulio de' Medici and Luigi de' Rossi*, 1518-1519: p.28 | **Rome: Sistine Chapel:** *The School of Athens*, 1511: p.28 | **Vienna: Kunsthistorisches Museum:** *Madonna with the Christ Child and Saint John the Baptist*, ca. 1506: p.3.

Verrocchio: Florence: Uffizi Gallery: *Baptism of Christ*, ca. 1475: p.6 (whole and detail) | **Florence: National Museum of Bargello:** *David*, ca. 1466-1469: p.6 | **Washington: National Gallery of Art:** *Lorenzo de' Medici*, ca. 1478: p.3.

Others: Bergamo: Accademia Carrara: Melone, *Portrait of a Gentleman (Cesare Borgia)*, ca. 1500-1524: p.23 | **Florence: Museo dell'Opera di Santa Maria del Fiore:** Brunelleschi, *Model of the lantern for the dome of Santa Maria del Fiore, Florence*, 1420: p.5 | **Los Angeles: Los Angeles County Museum of Art:** Sanzio Morghen, *Leonardo da Vinci*, 1817: p.4 | **Milan: Castle Trivulzio Library:** de Predis, *Portrait of Ludovico Sforza*, s.d.: p.10 | **New York: Metropolitan Museum of Art:** da Volterra, *Michelangelo*, ca. 1544: p.3, p.29 | **Paris: Musée du Louvre:** Rubens, *Drawing of The Battle of Anghiari, after Leonardo da Vinci*, ca. 1603: p.27; Clouet, *Francis I, King of France*, ca. 1530: p.31 | **Paris: Petit Palais:** Ingres, *Francis I receives the last breaths of Leonardo da Vinci*, 1818: p.31

Photographs:
Manoir du Clos-Lucé: p.5, p.6, p.30 | **Palazzo Vecchio:** p.27

Acknowledgments to everyone involved in the production of this book.

Did you enjoy this book?
Find all our books in our online shop

www.kateart.com